Over the past nine months I've been making visual text objects that i call *Speculative Poems*. Many have become starting points for morphological sequences, some more some less extended. When mIEKAL aND invited me to consider making work for Xerolage he was clear that he wanted a 'work' and not a collection of pieces. I took one of these Speculative Poems, number 33, 'The Tower,' as a starting point, and generated a sequence from that, then sat on the sidelines of its productivity while other commitments drove past. I came back to 'The Tower' a couple of months later, made more variations and then feeling daunted by selection generated a still further bunch, until i had upwards of 300 images all drawn from a common starting point.

I use a computer as a tool to encourage one image to become another image, often until the line falls dead and my interest leaves me. Page 1 is the starting image, labeled 'The Tower,' drawn from the frontispiece of a book published in 1639. I have a substantive documentary poetics project under the title 1639, that asks all manner of questions about documents and power. Page 2 generated the humpty dumpty figure from which the title grew. As i cut from and cropped in and filtered differing objects in the series, so an increasing number of beasts emerged. This selection tries to convey a sense of the entire series while cutting to a necessary quick. Sometimes the jumps are fierce and the more obvious history of association in shape might be submerged. Consider this book a drill into morphological sequence, an edit from corral to distinction.

In the mid 1970s I had the great fortune to work closely on a day-to-day basis with Bob Cobbing and Bill Griffiths, running an open access print shop helping poet-publishers in London at what was then the Poetry Society and this set of images does bear some kinship to what Cobbing got up to with a photocopier in terms of manipulating scale and working with digital artifacts of a copying and rendering process. Bob and Bill and i used a mix of print technologies, and together with other members of the Consortium of London Presses such as Allen Fisher, Ulli Freer and Lawrence Upton we exploited the printing process for creative purposes. The entanglement of print, politics and procedure have stuck with me since. This book is for them, and for Erin without whom nothing.

ISBN-10: 1-936687-50-X
ISBN-13: 978-1-936687-50-3

Xerolage 70 First Edition published 2018   ISSN 1557-0983
Visual poetry, copy art & collage graphics, each issue devoted to the work of one artist. Xerolage is a word coined by mIEKAL aND to suggest the world of 8.5 x 11 art propagated by xerox technology, "The mimeo of the 80s." The primary investigation of this magazine is how collage technique of 20th century art, typography, computer graphics, visual & concrete poetry movements & the art of the xerox have been combined. 8.5x11, 24 pages each. Subscriptions $24/4 issues. For overseas delivery, add $15 for airmail printed matter.

Back issues $6.00 each.

Xexoxial Editions, 10375 Cty Hway Alphabet, LaFarge, WI 54639
www.xexoxial.org | perspicacity@xexoxial.org

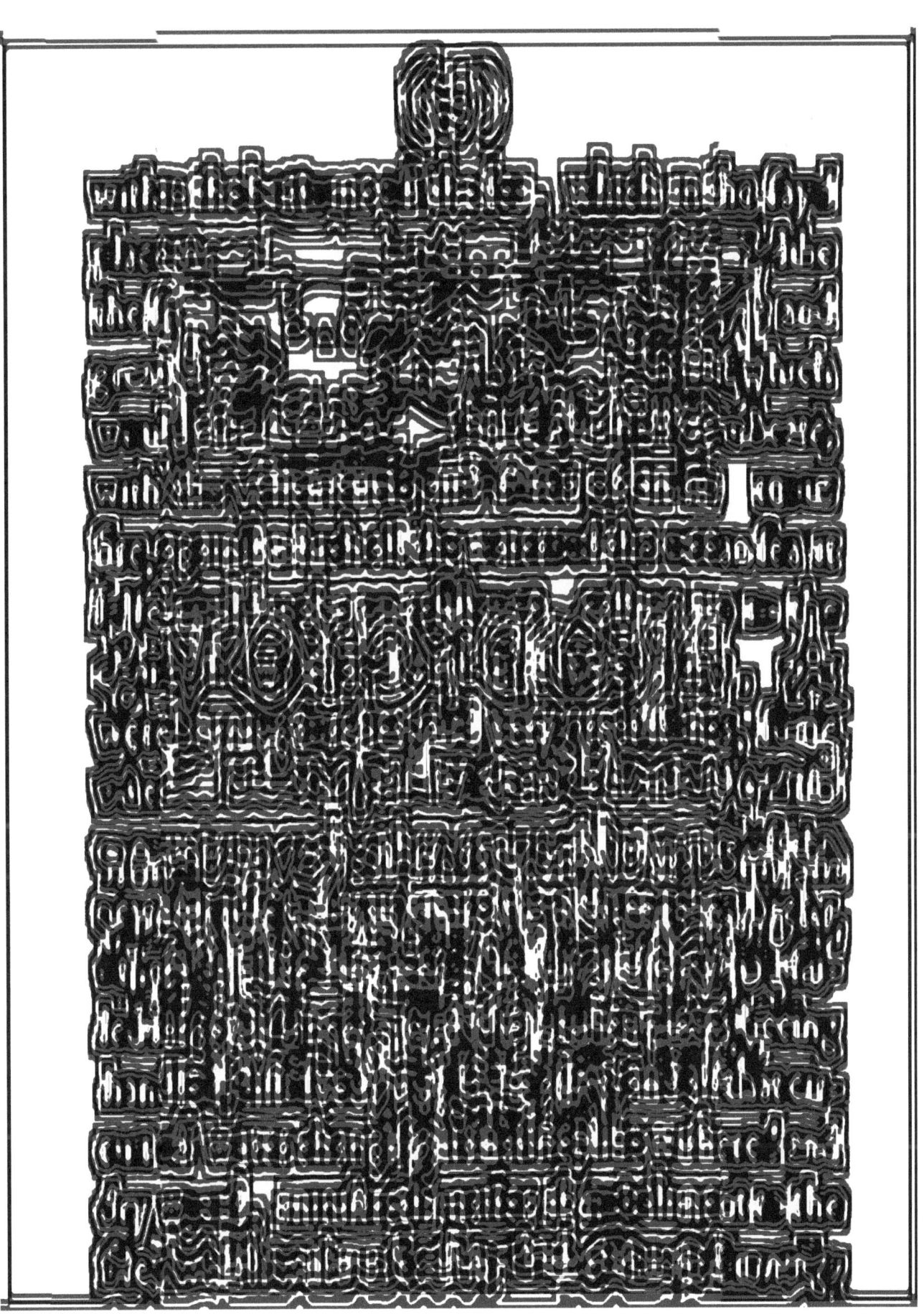

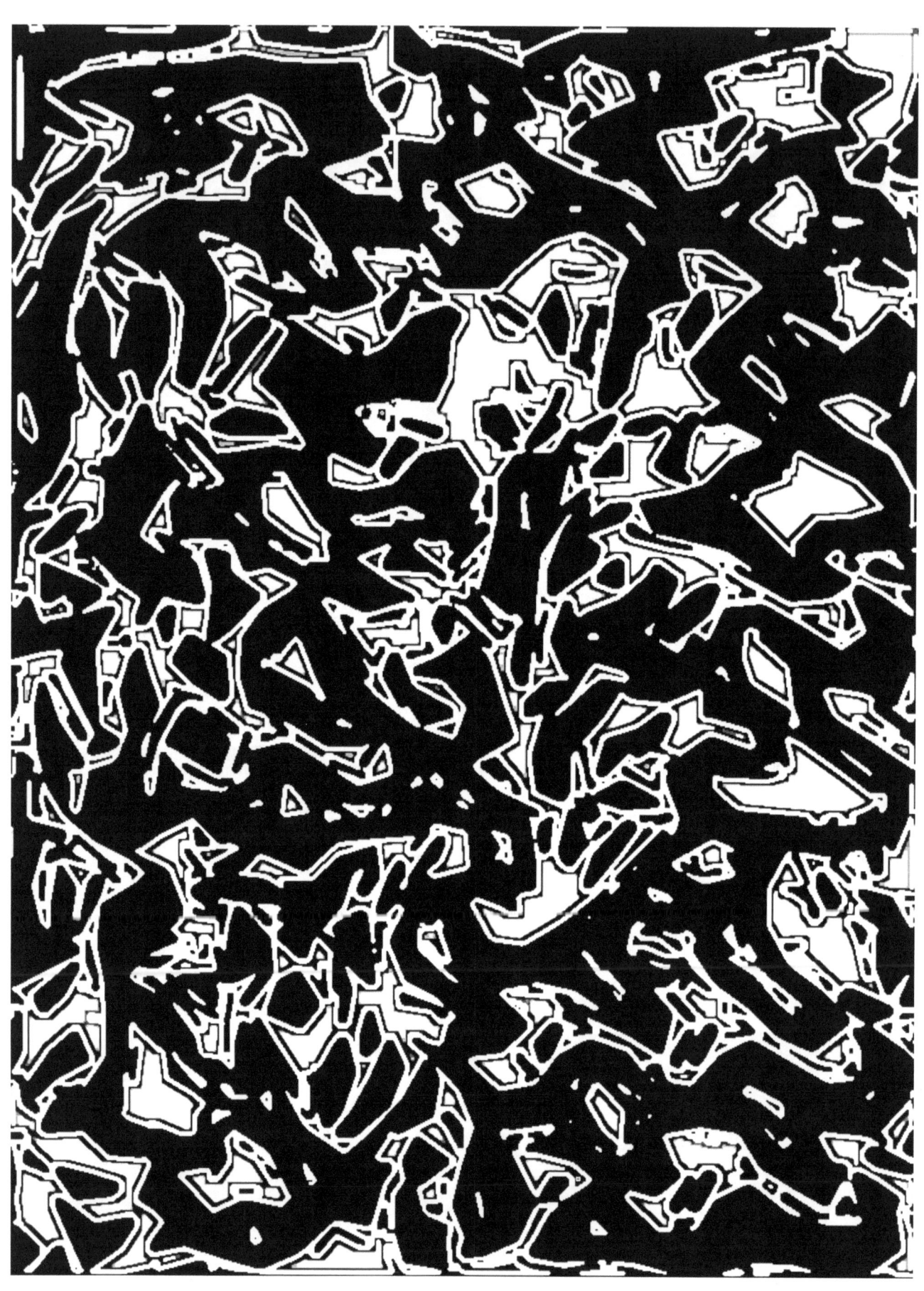

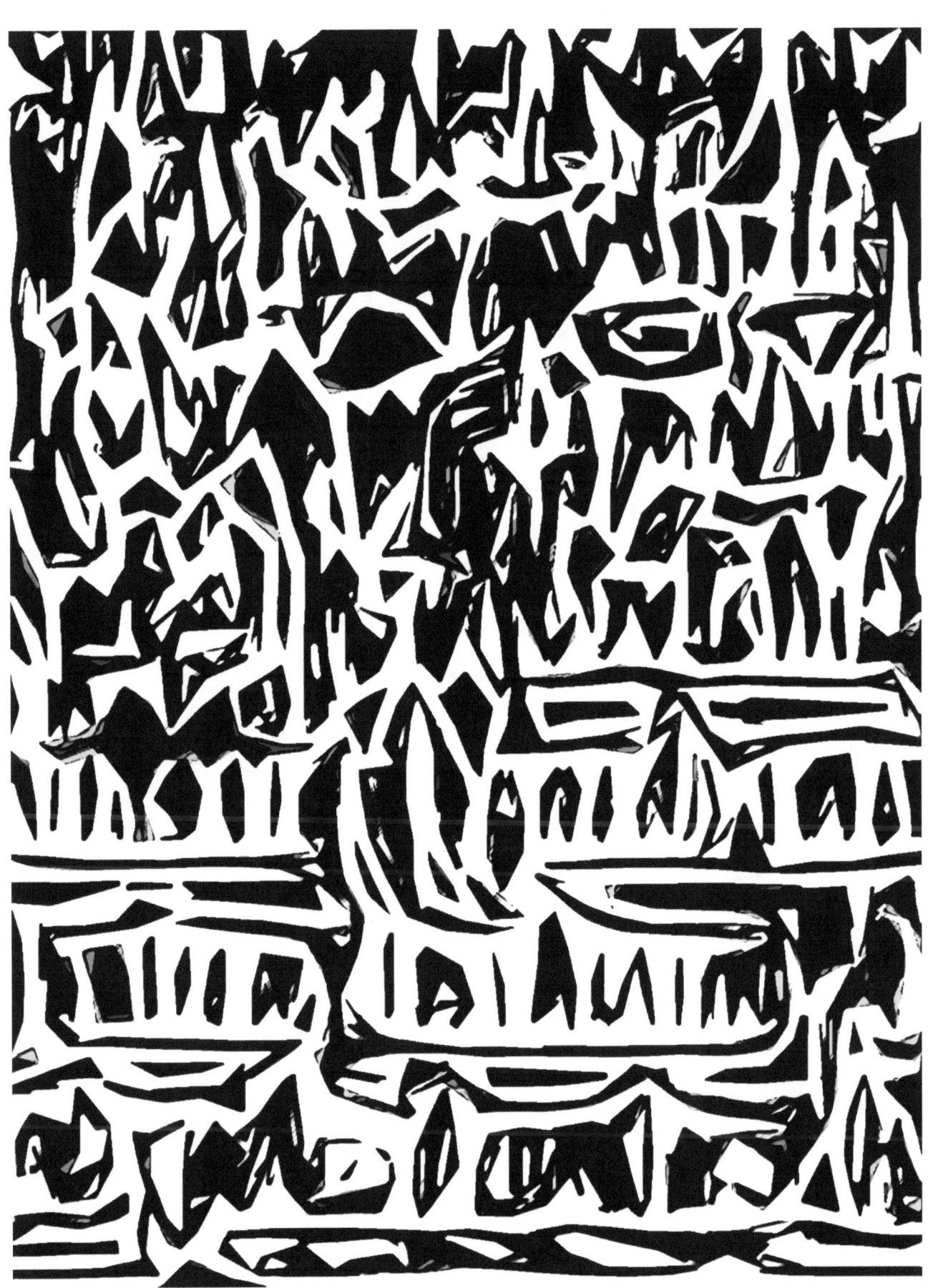

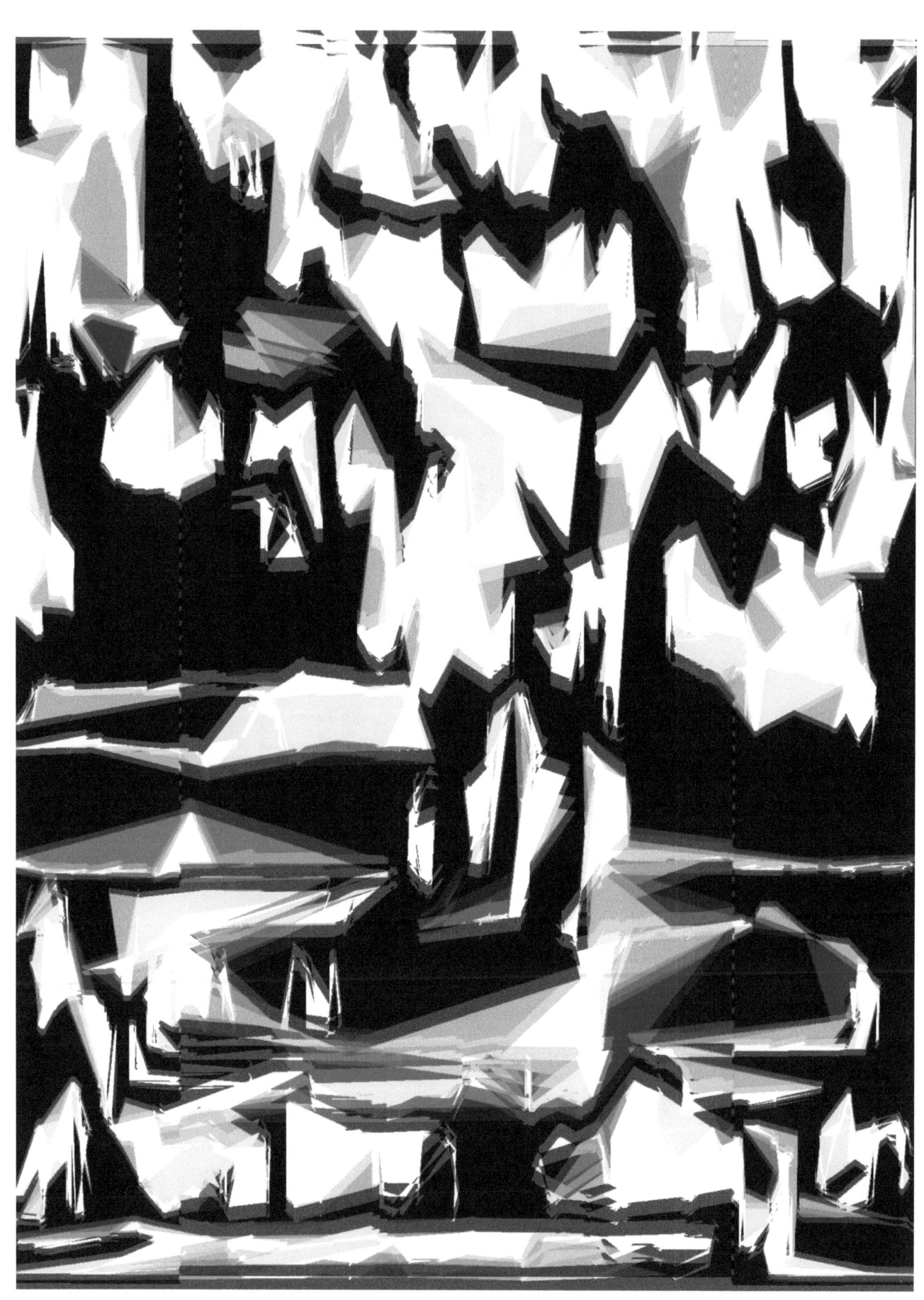

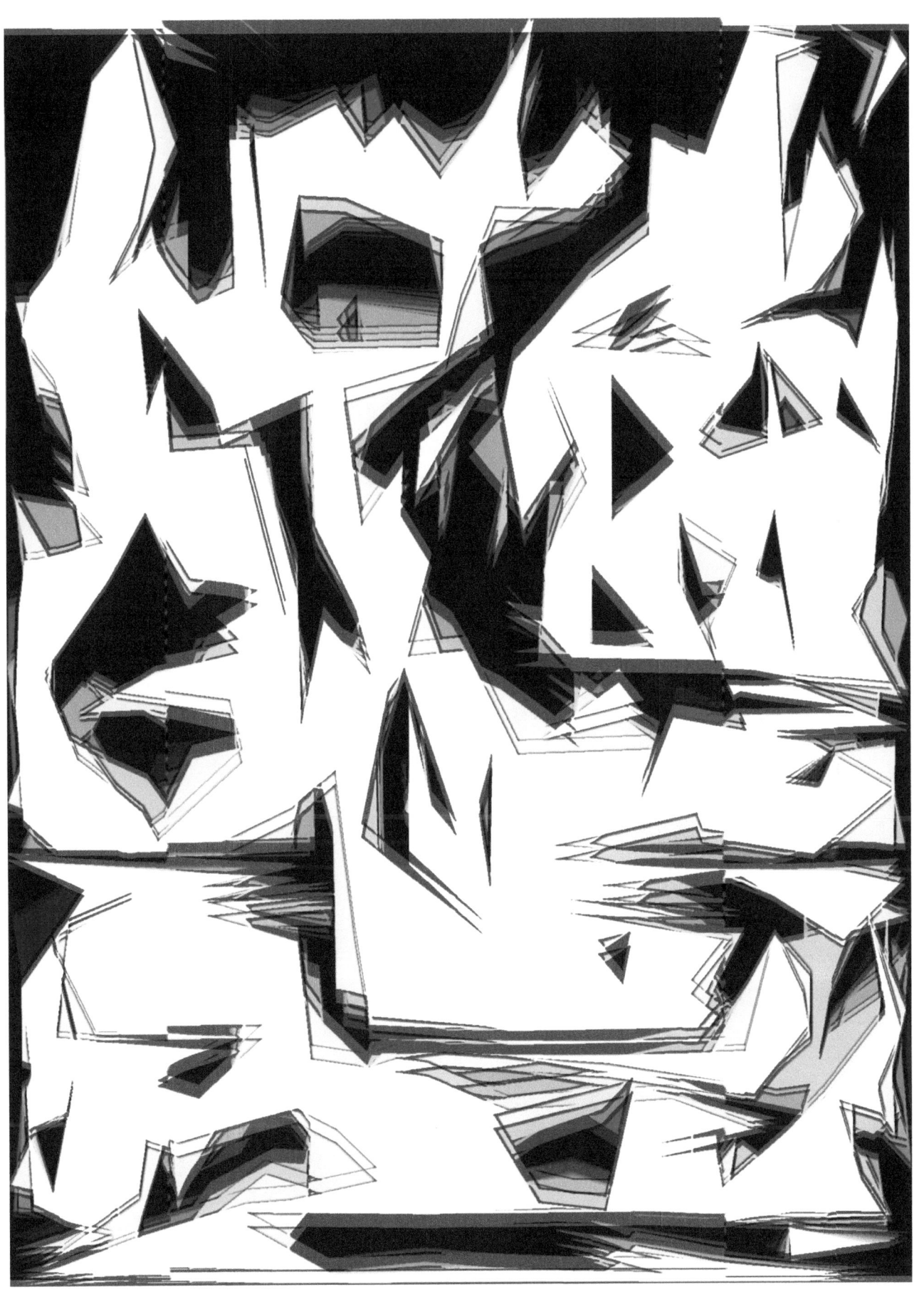

cris cheek

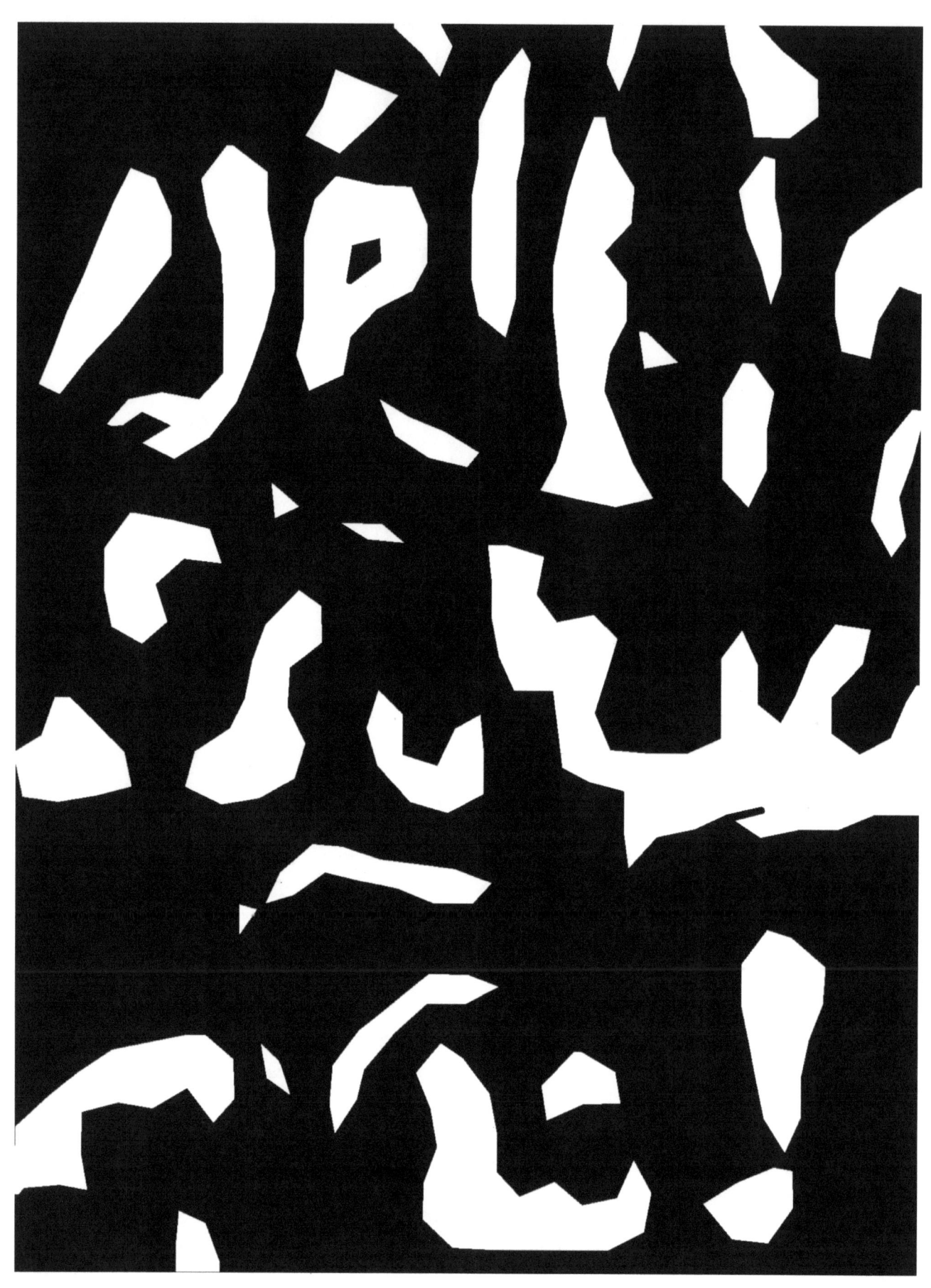

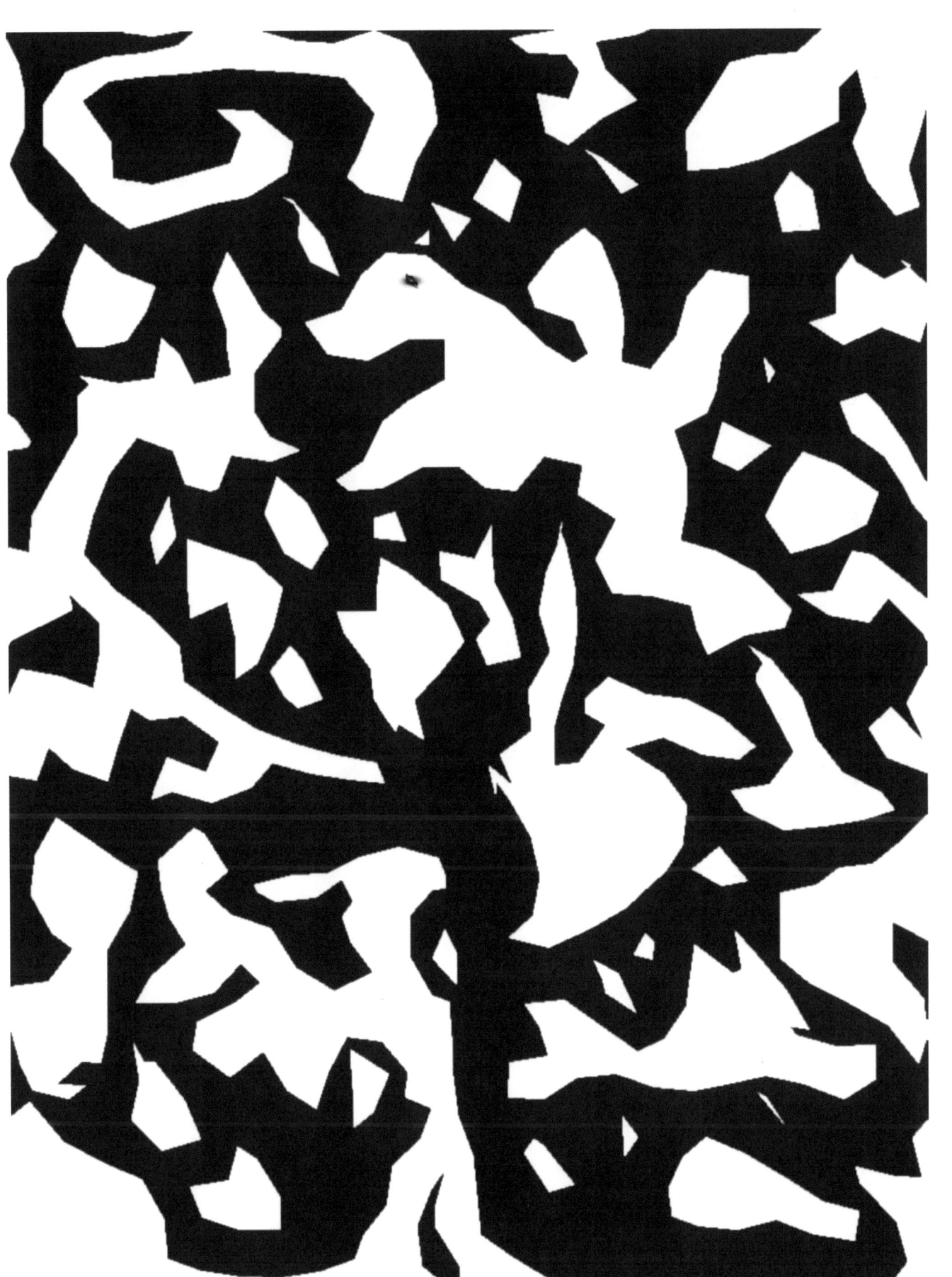

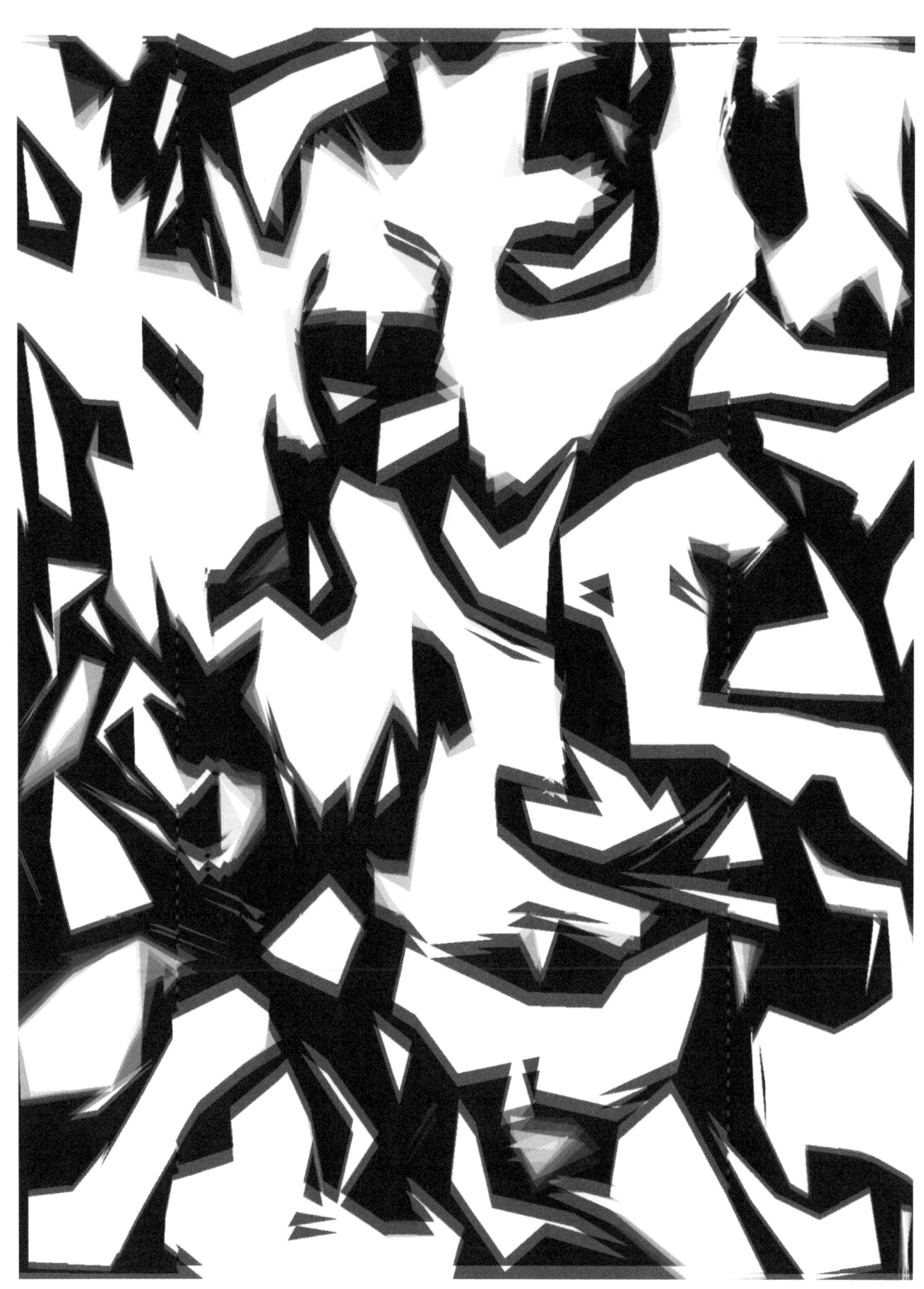

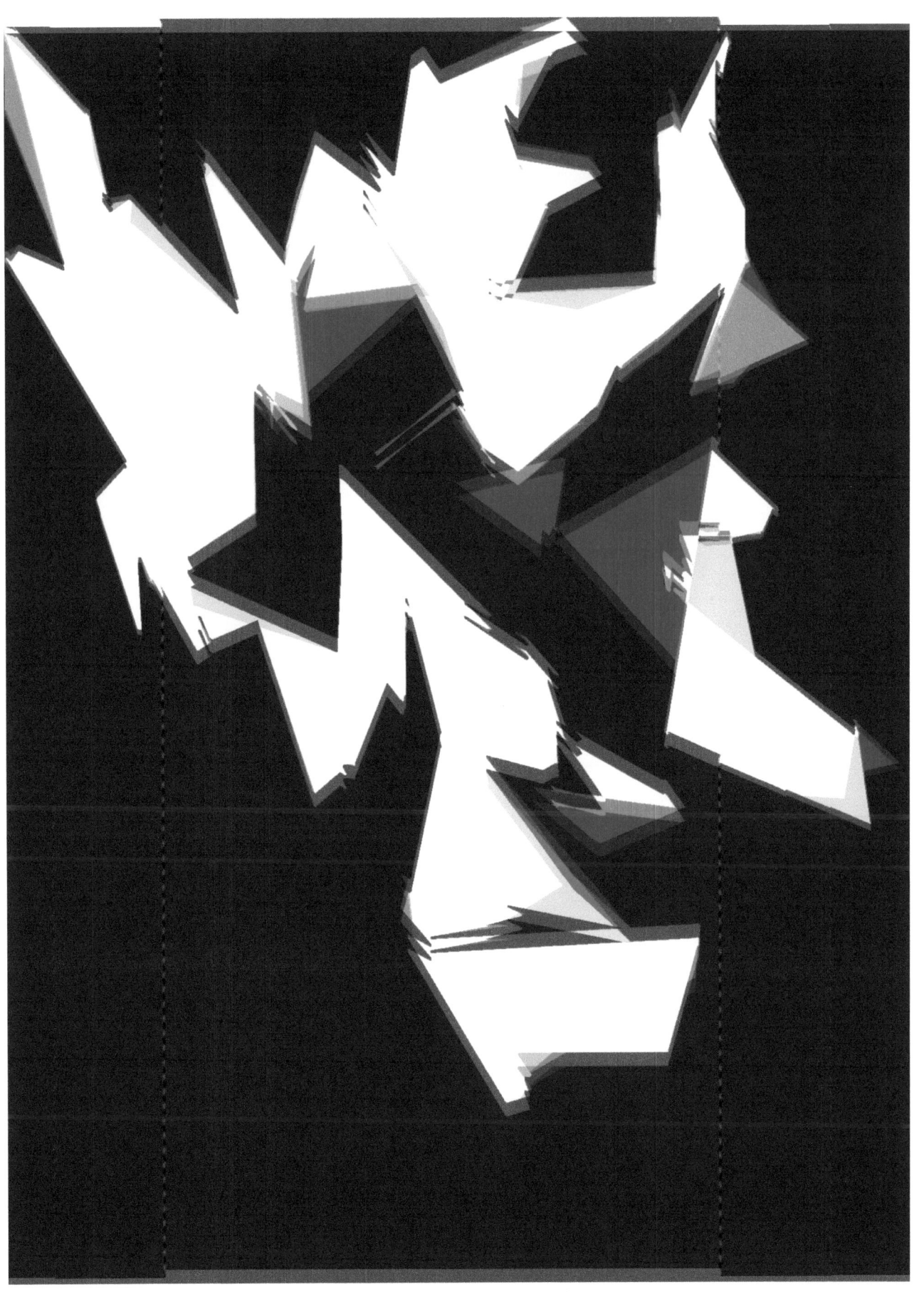

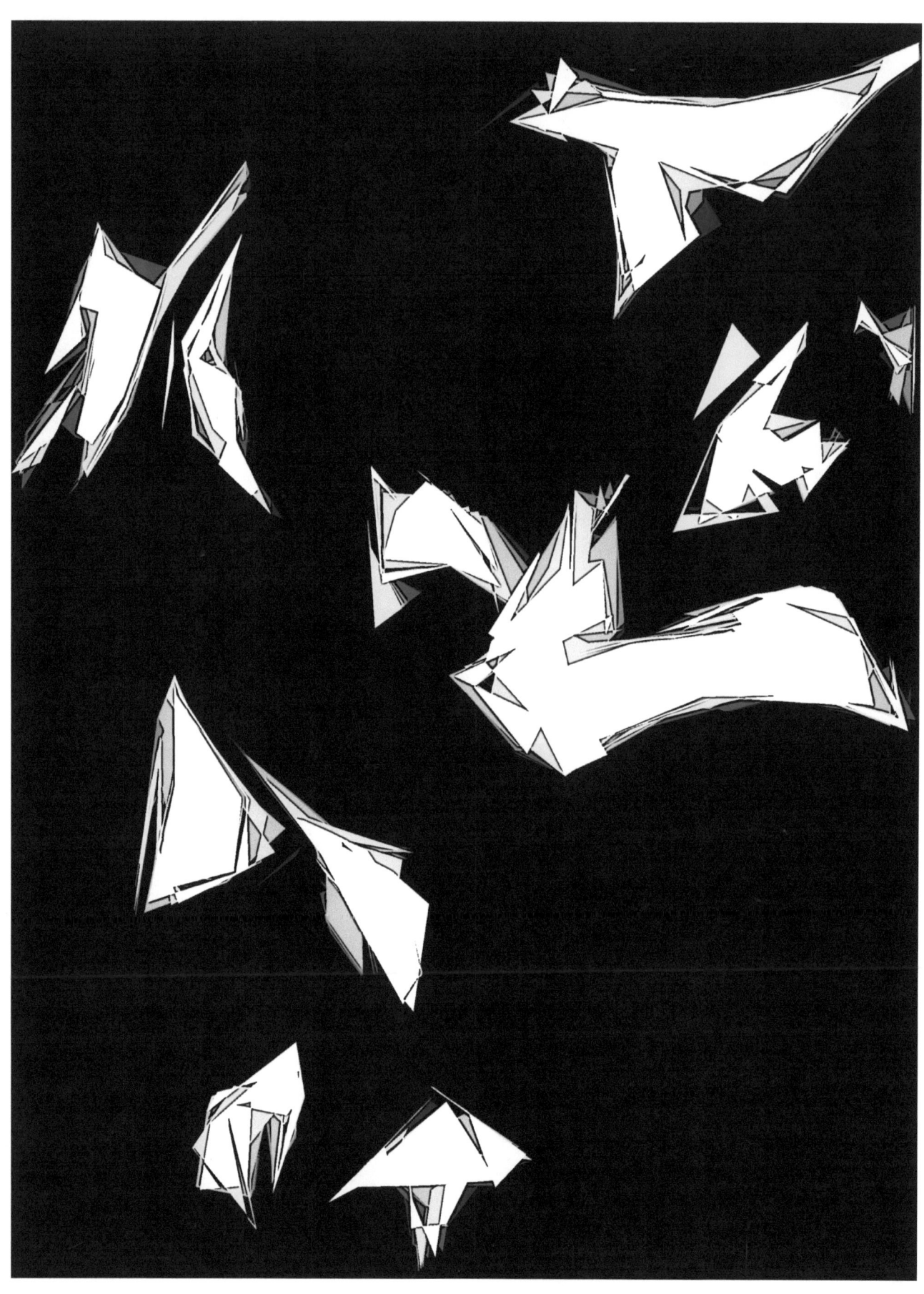

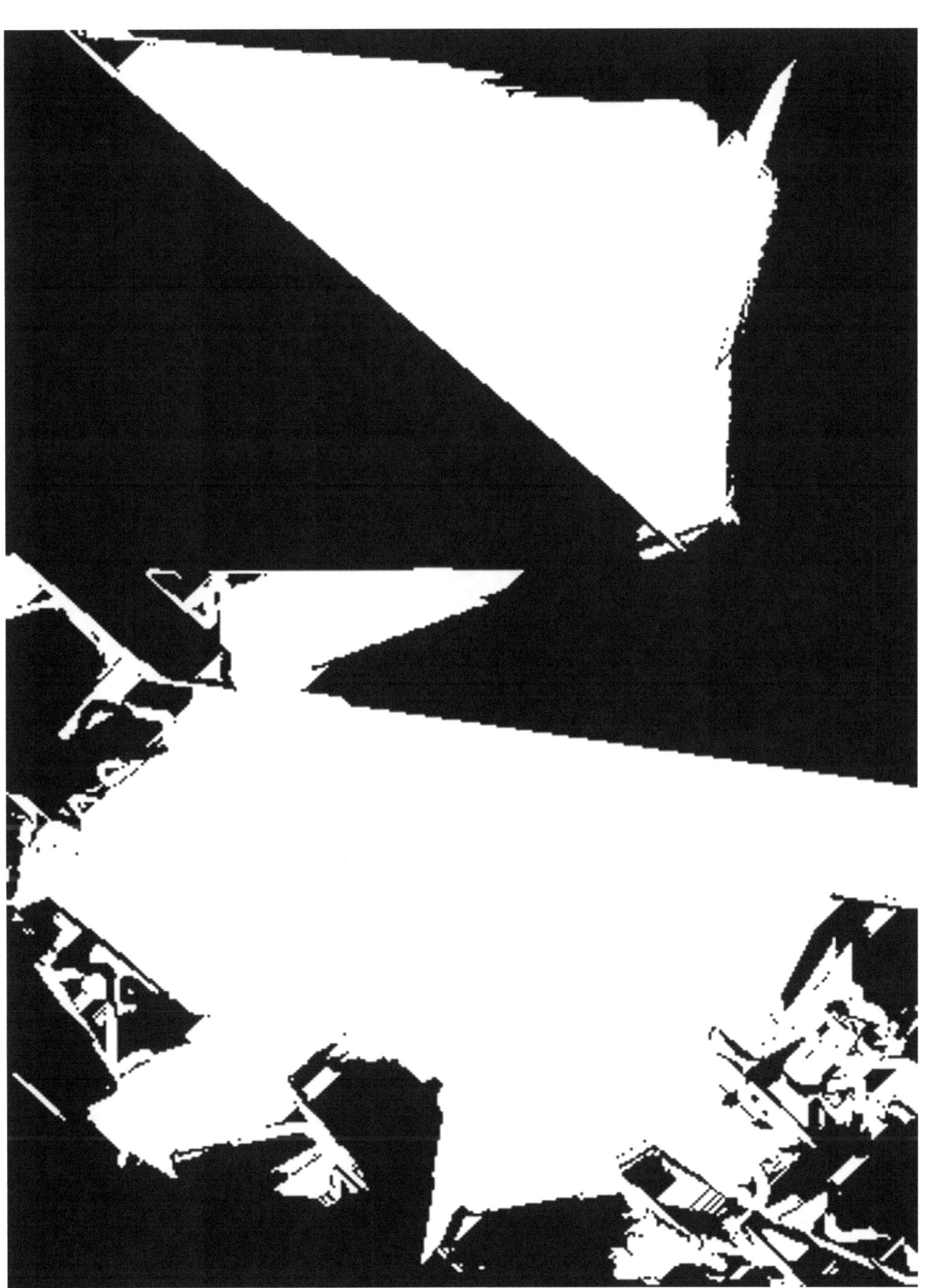

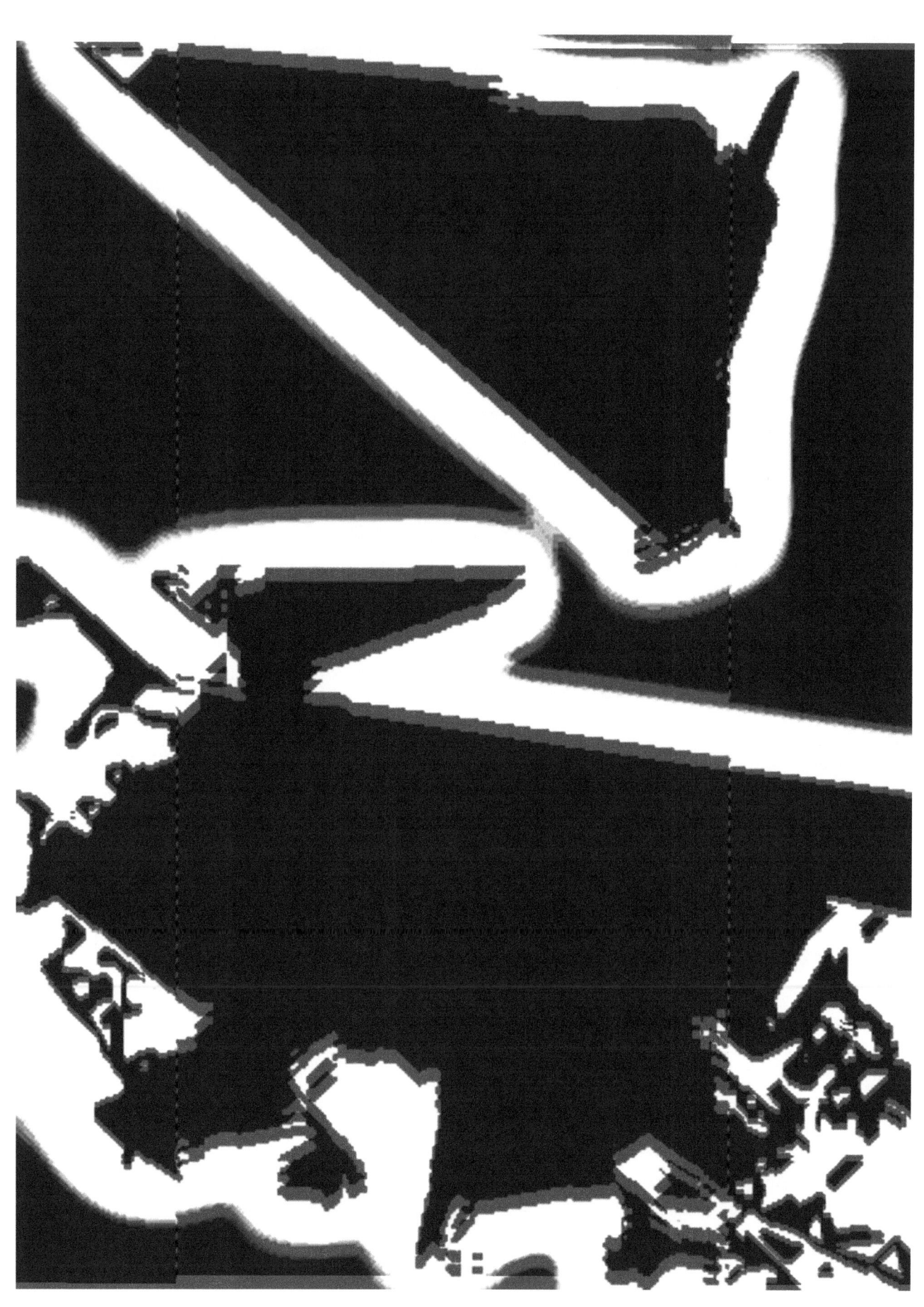

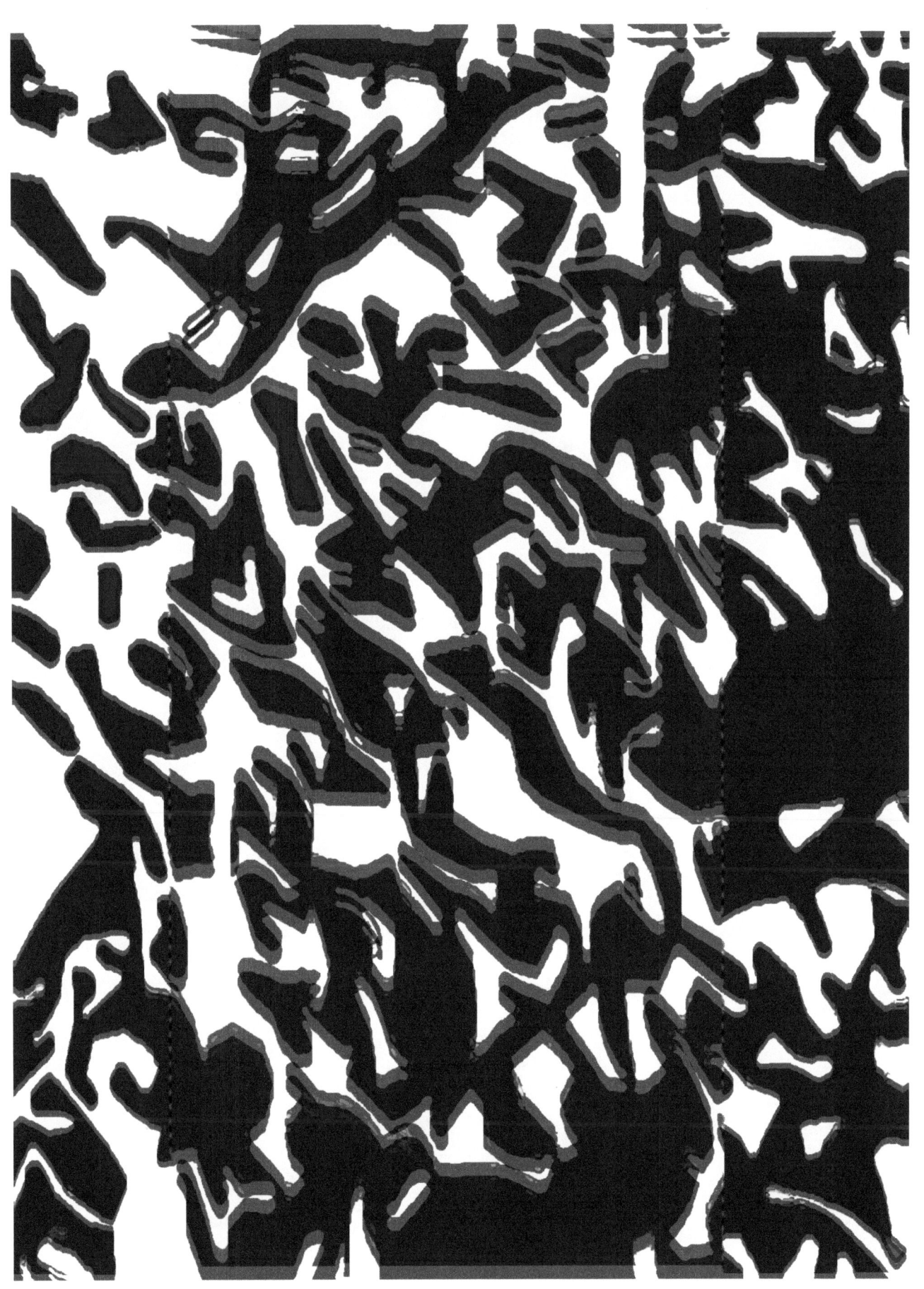

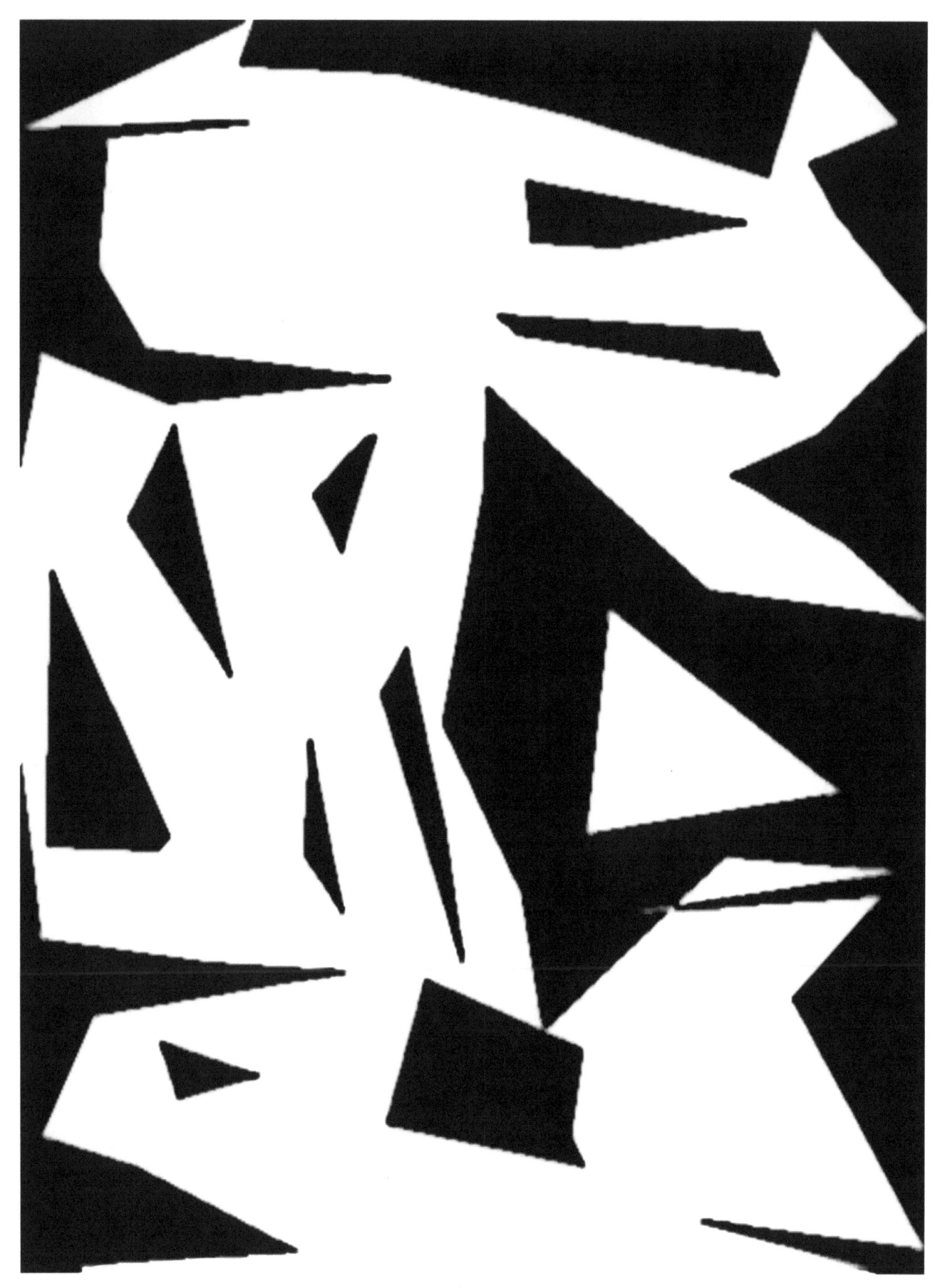

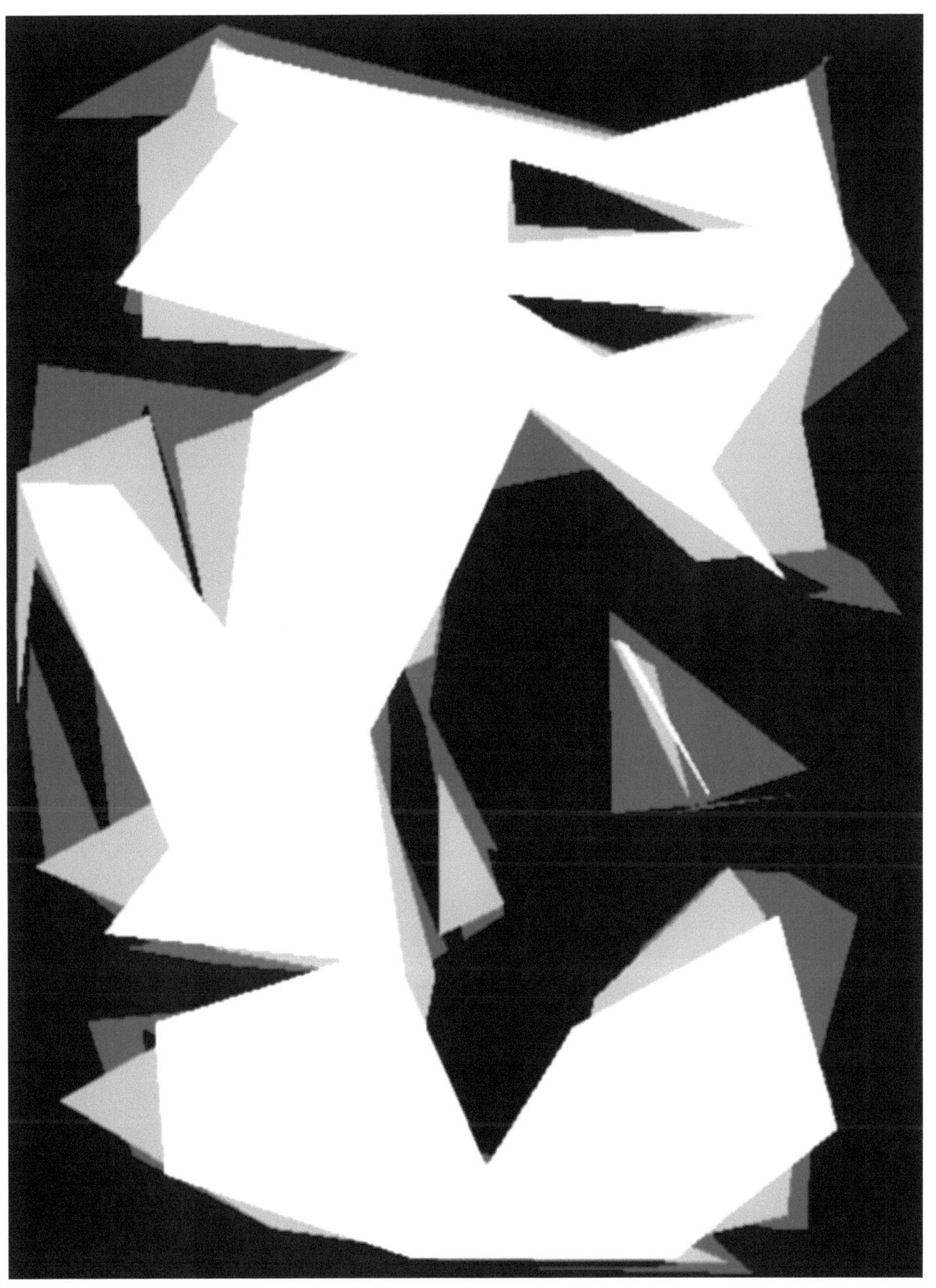

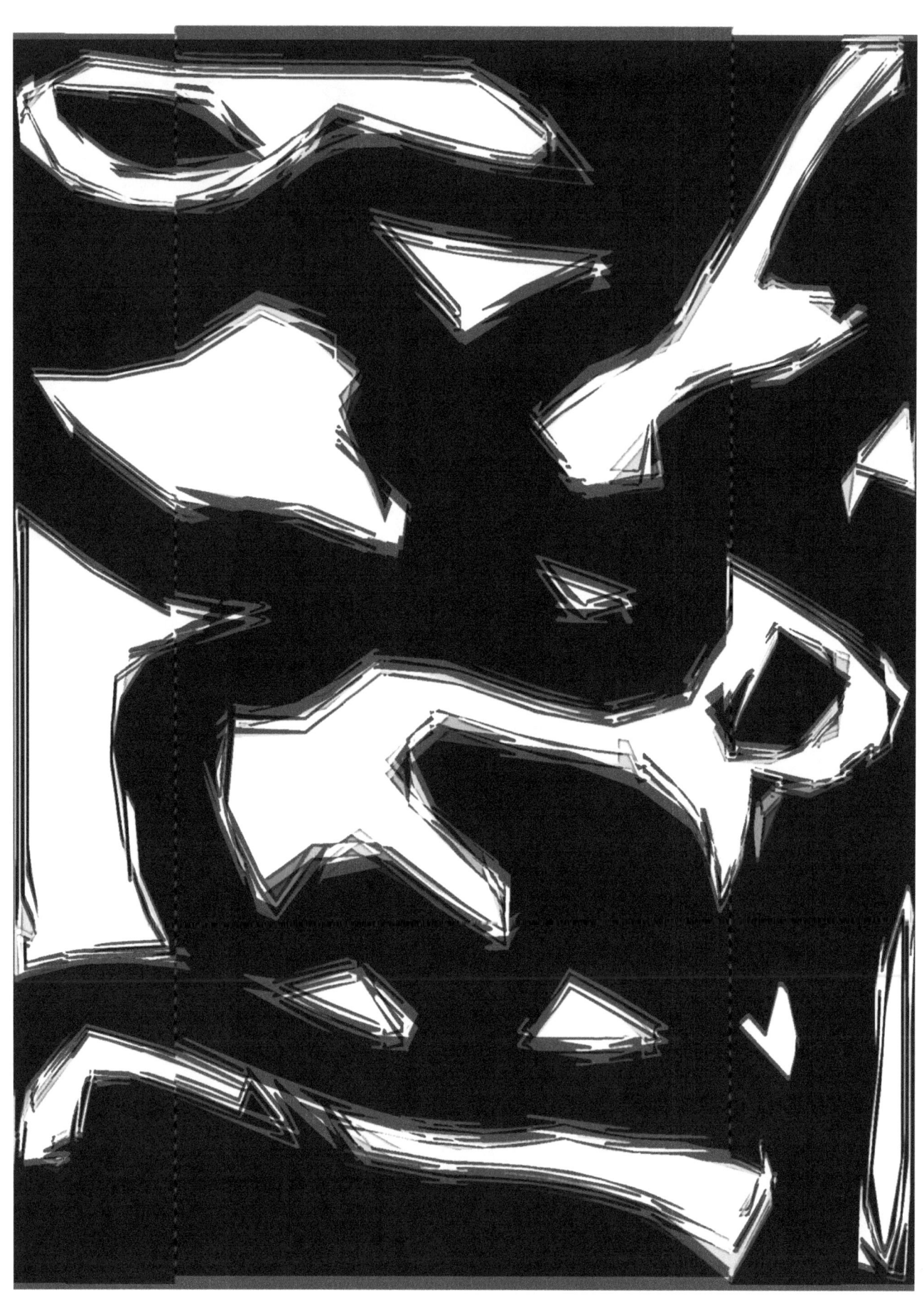

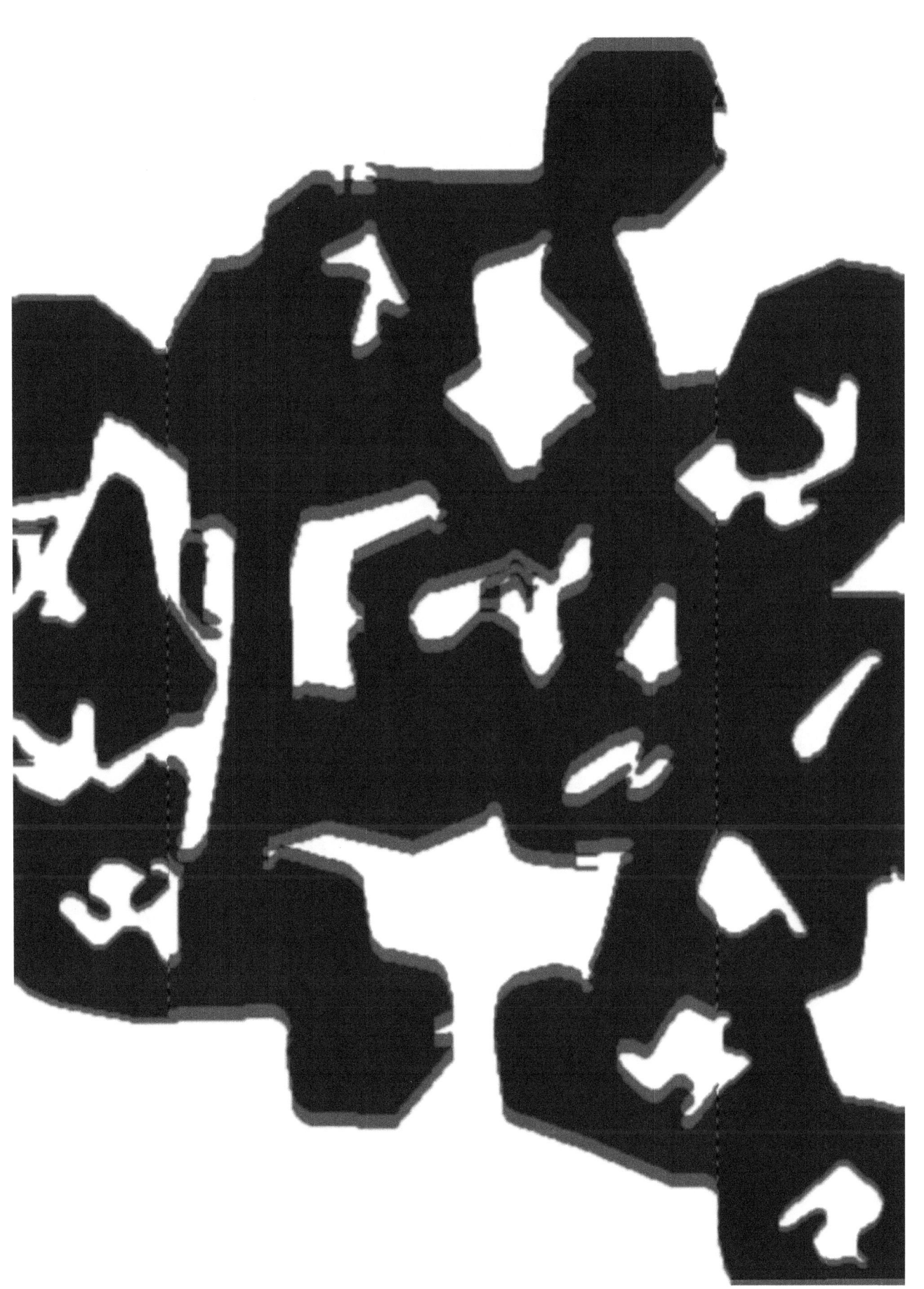

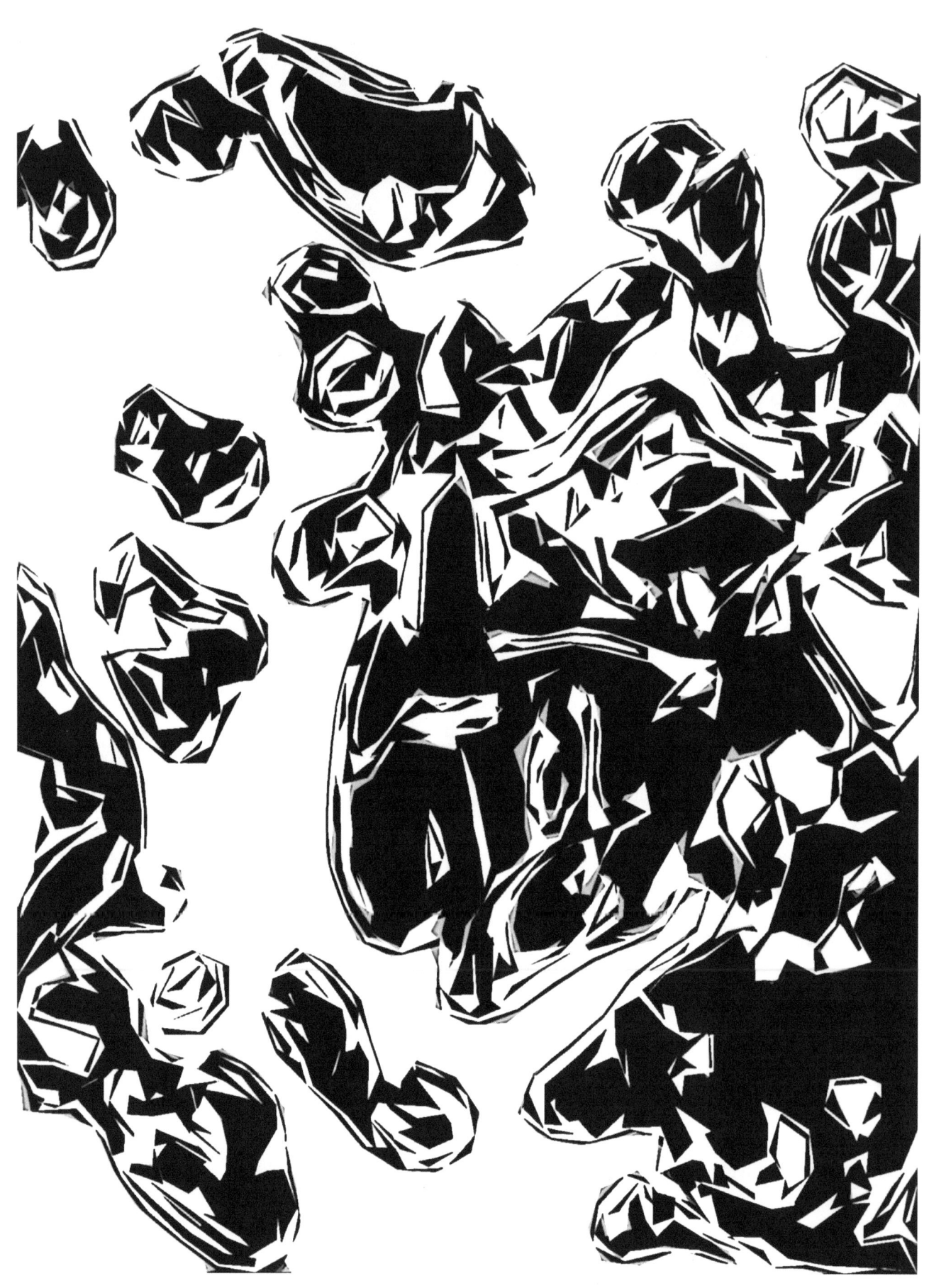

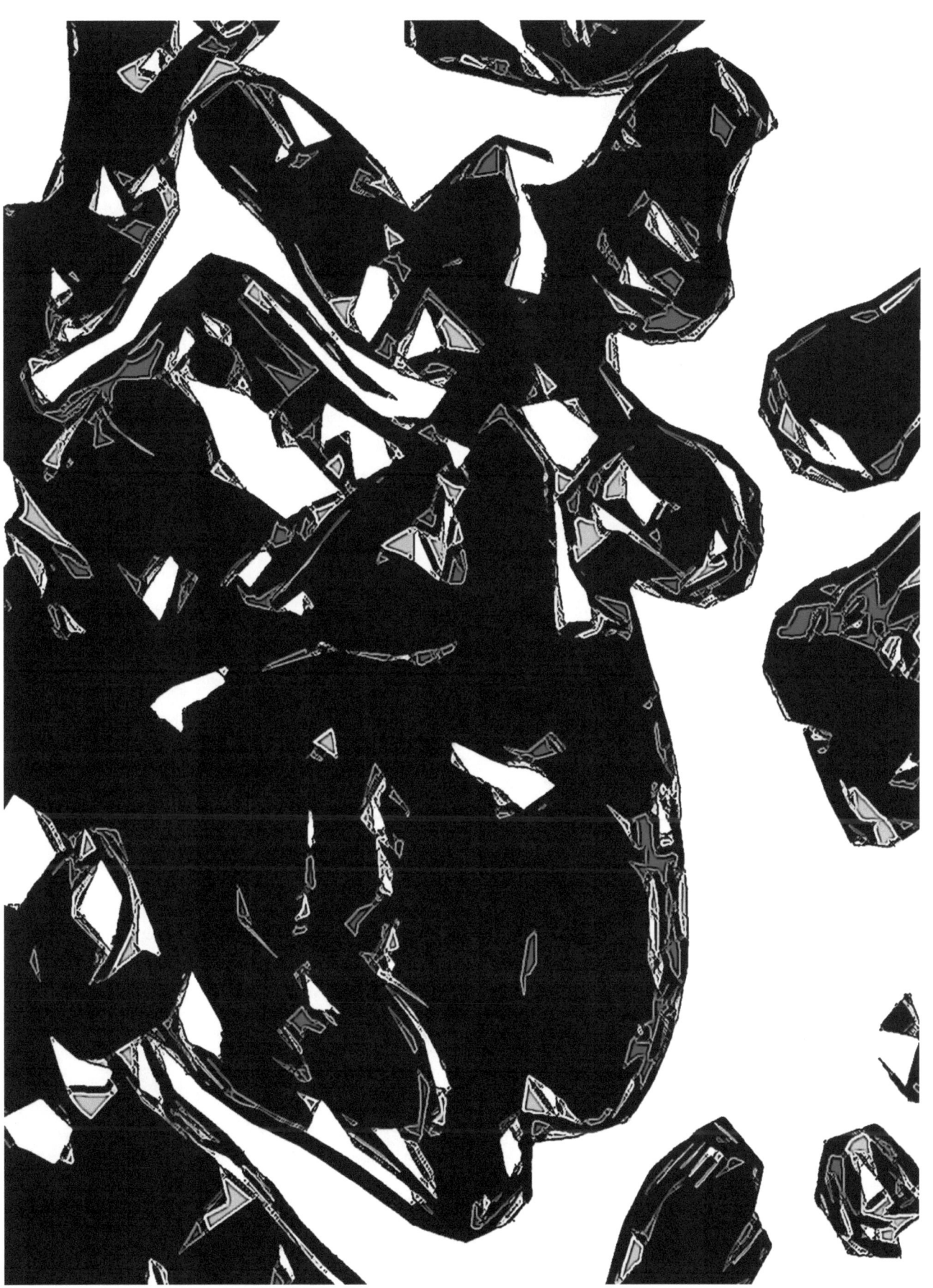

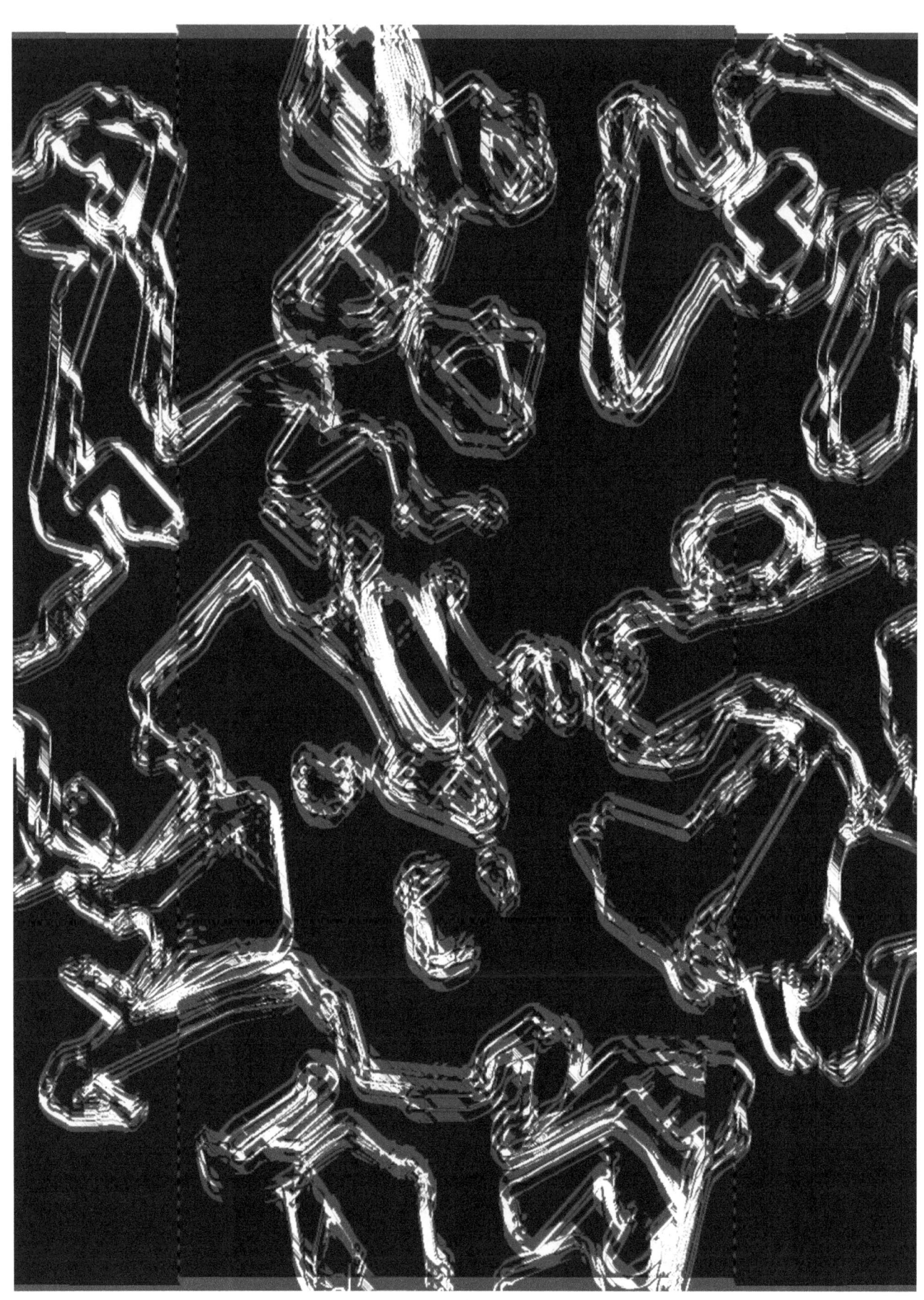

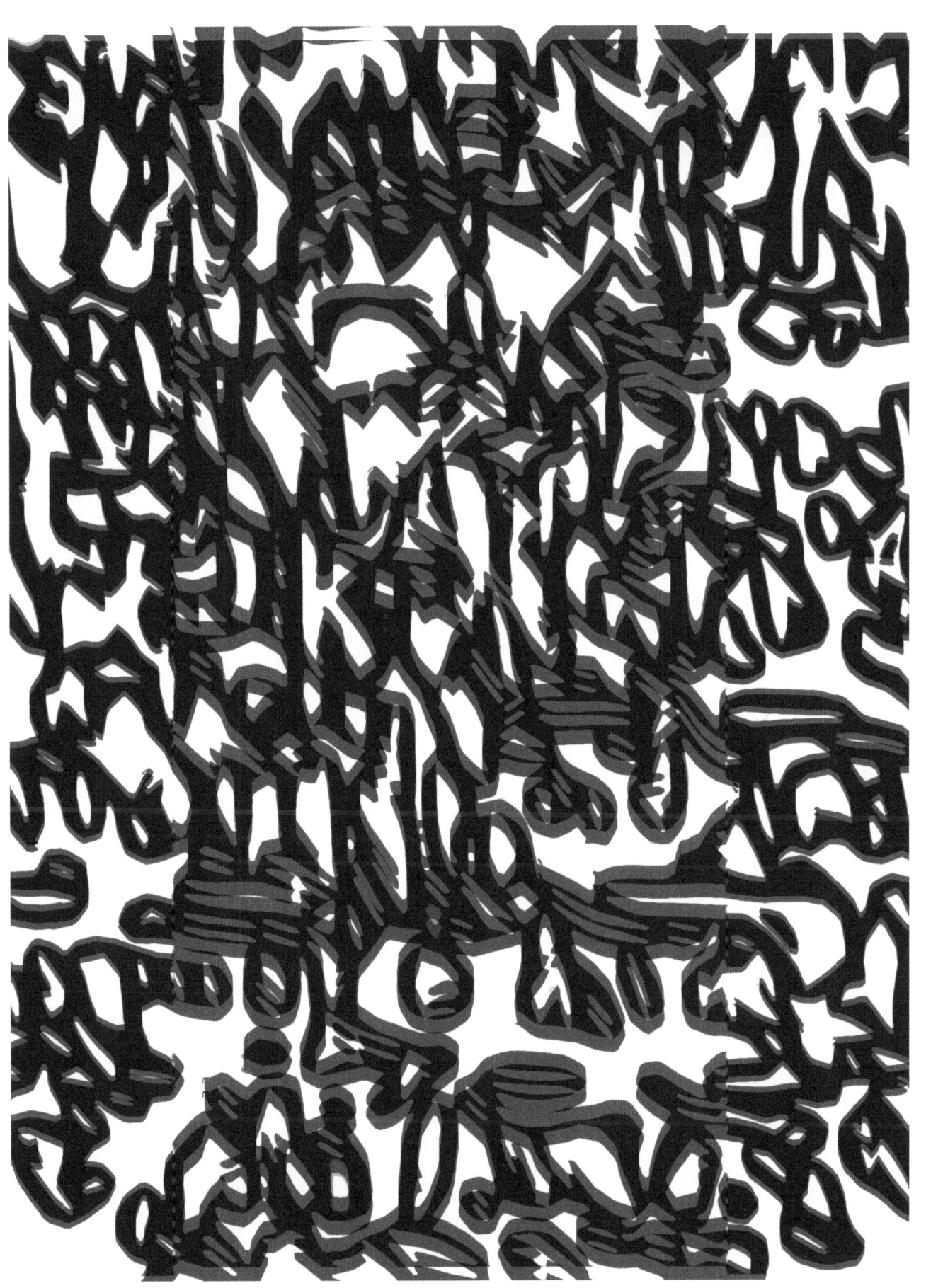

cris cheek

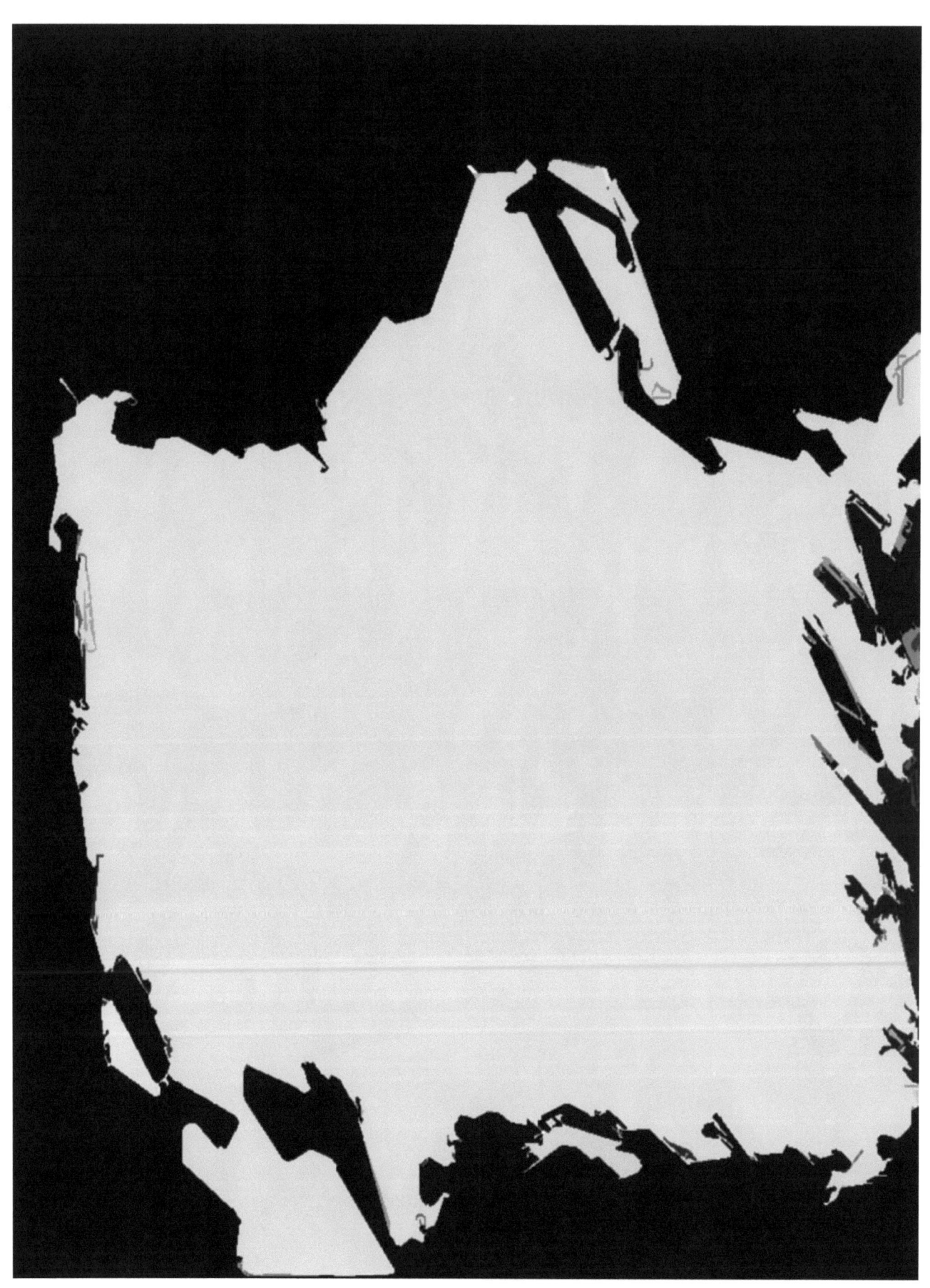

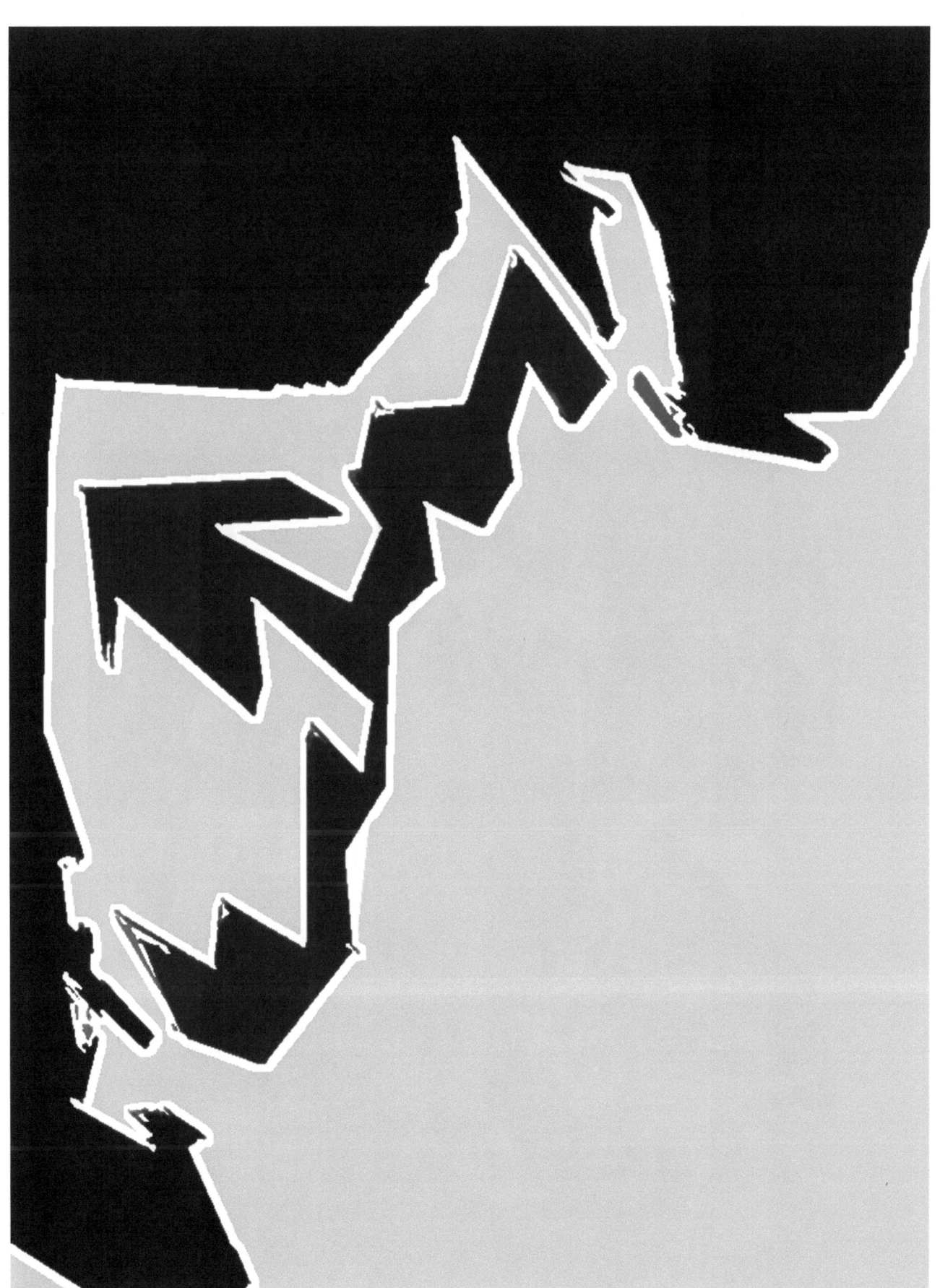

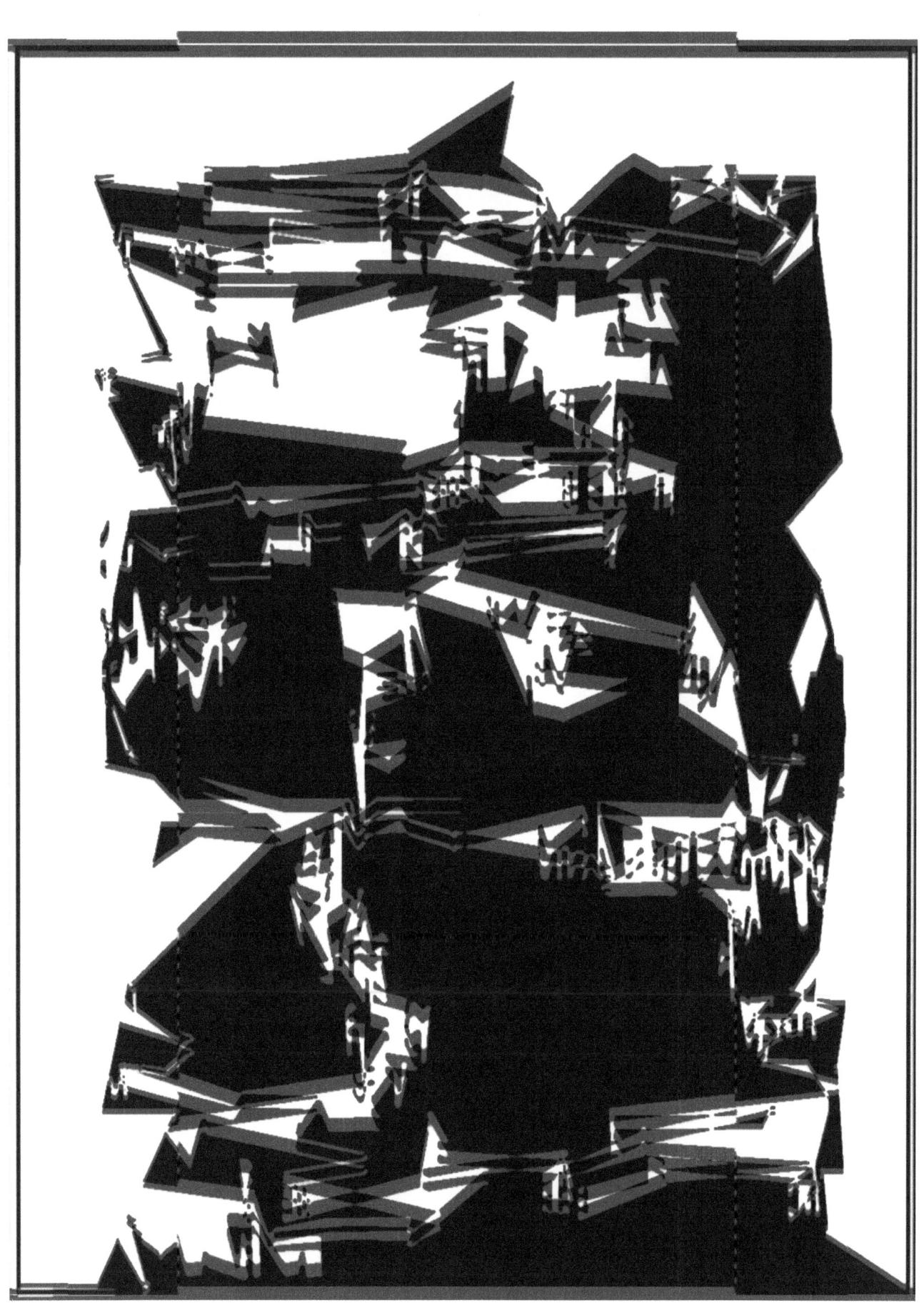

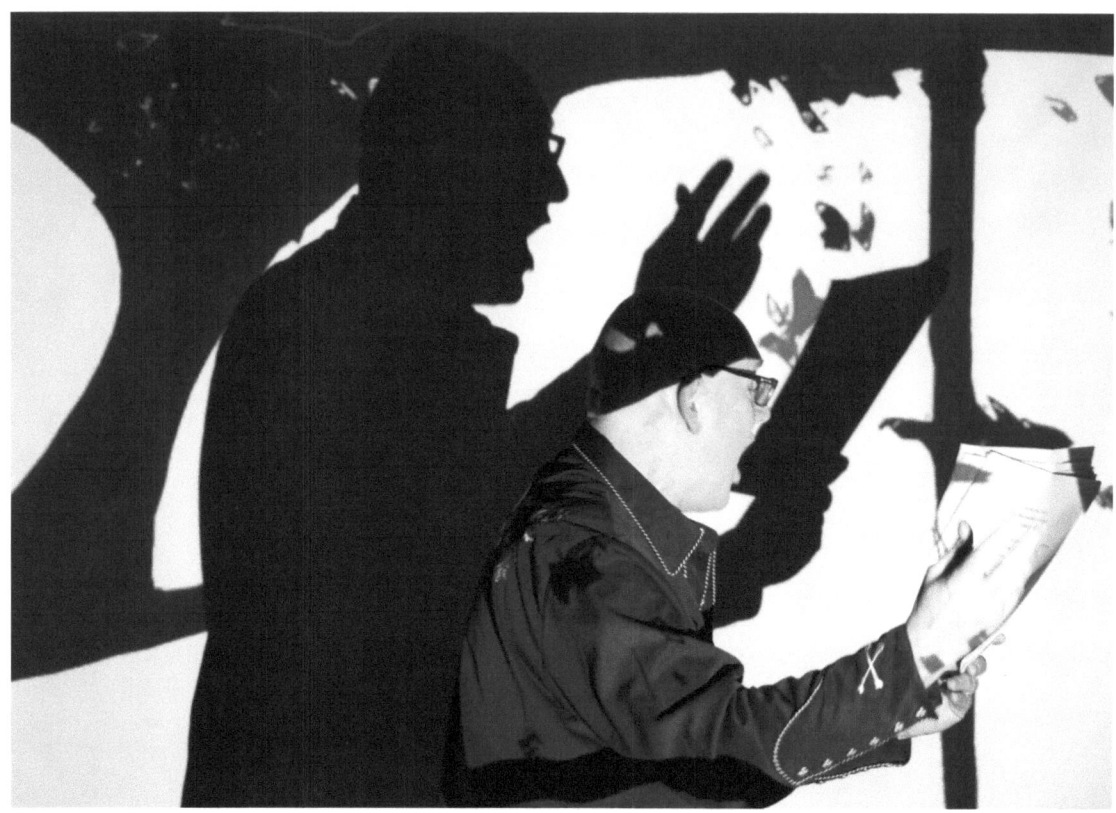

photo by Erin Edwards

cris cheek is a documentary performance writer, sound composer and photographer. He worked alongside Bob Cobbing and Bill Griffiths with the Consortium of London Presses in the mid 1970s to run a thriving open access print shop for *little press* poets. In 1981 he co-founded a collective movement-based performance resource in the east end of London at Chisenhale Dance Space, working with choreographers, musicians and performance artists to make collaborations based in embodied movement. cris taught Performance Writing at Dartington College of Arts (1995-2002), played music with Sianed Jones and Philip Jeck as *Slant*, collaborated on site-responsive works about value and recycling with *Things Not Worth Keeping* and has been a professor at Miami University in Ohio since 2005, currently living in Cincinnati. Most recent publications are *the church, the school, the beer* (Critical Documents, 2007), *part: short life housing* (The Gig, 2009) and *pickles & jams* (BlazeVOX Books, 2017). He podcasts with Mack Hagood as Phantom Power: sounds about sound.

www.ingramcontent.com/pod-product-compliance
Lightning Source LLC
Chambersburg PA
CBHW051942210526
45473CB00006B/2341